Narcissism Unleashed!

BY JEFFREY POWELL

The Ultimate Guide to Understanding the Mind of a Narcissist, Sociopath and Psychopath!

3rd Edition

Table of Contents

Introduction

I want to thank you and congratulate you for downloading the book, *"Narcissism Unleashed: The Ultimate Guide to Understanding the Mind of a Narcissist, Sociopath and Psychopath!"*.

This book contains proven steps and strategies on how to distinguish between a narcissist, sociopath and psychopath. These three personality disorders have attracted attention over the years due to their sinister connotations. Through this book, you should be able to fully understand the mind of the people who fall within these categories and the REAL role that they play in today's society.

Crime shows often portray narcissists, sociopaths and psychopaths as the bad guys prone to doing heinous activities – but are they really? You might be surprised! This book will offer you in-depth information about the mind of a narcissist, psychopath and sociopath. Find out what makes them tick and whether society's portrayal of these disorders is accurate. If you're a true crime fan, interested in human psychology is simply curious about these disorders – this is the book for you!

Thanks again for purchasing this book, I hope you enjoy it!

Chapter 1: Narcissism – An Overview

If you're a fan of true crime or happen to love watching crime shows like *CSI* and *Criminal Minds*, chances are you've heard of the terms narcissists, sociopath and psychopath used in reference to murder suspects. But what exactly do they mean? Although narcissism is fairly easy to distinct, the terms sociopath and psychopath are often confused by many people.

Narcissism

In simple terms, narcissism is defined as an extreme love for oneself. The term was derived from the name *Narcissus,* a character in Greek Mythology who fell in love with his own image. People who have this personality disorder are often preoccupied with their own triumphs and self-importance, even if there's no proper cause. They expect to be treated as special and believe that they are the object of envy for many. Famous people rumored to be narcissist include: Adolf Hitler, Paris Hilton and Joseph Stalin.

It is said that 1% of the world's population are narcissists although this hasn't been confirmed. What is sure though is that Narcissistic Personality Disorder (NPD) isn't just exhibited by celebrities or people in the limelight. *Megalomania* was the first word coined to describe narcissism, introduced around 1968.

One thing most people don't realize is that narcissism stems from a personality trait that every person has: ego or how you see your level of importance. Ego is actually an important aspect of every mentally healthy individual.

Narcissists however, have pushed the boundaries to its limits, displaying extreme self-love or what is often termed as *egomania*.

Symptoms of Narcissism

Mental health professionals often look for 9 distinct characteristics associated with NPD. Note though that these signs are usually present in many people but those without the disorder are often capable of controlling the problem. Therefore, people with NPD often showcase these signs in extreme proportions:

1. An inflated sense of self-esteem, often believing that their opinions, beliefs and strategies are far superior to those of others.

2. Acts as if they are unique or deserve special treatment from others. Narcissists believe that no one else understands them aside from other special people.

3. Constantly thinks about achieving great success in terms of power, attractiveness, and intelligence. In most cases, they are more preoccupied with thoughts of success rather than facing real-life triumphs and failures.

4. Fails to sympathize with other people, often ignoring others in a bid to keep attention. Individuals with NPD have a hard time listening to others and would usually steer the conversation back to them. They seek admiration from others and believe that they are the source of envy for many.

5. Extreme feelings of entitlement. Narcissists are of the belief that due to their "special" status, the rules and guidelines do not apply to them.

6. They are more likely to exploit others while getting all the rewards and recognition themselves. This is done with zero guilt or regret as they believe themselves to be perfectly deserving of the praise. More often than not, narcissists hate working towards a goal because they believe that this common task is beneath them.

7. Lack of empathy or compassion for others. Practically all narcissists are incapable of understanding or connecting with other people on an emotional level. However, they are capable of faking empathy should the need arise.

8. Often criticize others in an effort to put them down. This type of behavior bolsters their self-esteem, leading to unwarranted arrogance.

9. Tend to display envy when others have more fame, fortune, appeal or anything else they desire. This envy is often displayed through distaste, contempt and insults that are hard to hide for the narcissists mind. More often than not, people with NPD prefer to be the ones who inspire envy.

Other signs that might be displayed by a narcissistic mind include but are not limited to the following:

- Tends to exaggerate their triumphs and achievements

- Displays extreme cases of jealousy

- Consider themselves highly skilled in whatever they do, most especially when it comes to romantic situations

- Easily feels rejected and often magnifies situations of rejection

- Extreme emotional response to humiliation which usually includes anger, shame or humiliation

Theories on Causes

There is no exact cause for Narcissistic Personality Disorder although there have been some theories on the matter. What it boils down to however is: nature and nurture. Some experts argue that there's a strong genetic link for narcissism, meaning that a family member diagnosed with the condition likely has another family member with the same.

Nurture factors to narcissism have also been pointed out, citing "over-attention" provided to the person during childhood. Overly pampered children set with high expectations at an early time in their life can lead to self-centered tendencies. On the other end of the spectrum however, there are also instances when abused children grow up to be narcissists.

Diagnosis of Narcissism

Narcissistic Personality Disorder is diagnosed using DSM-5 (Diagnostic and Statistical Manual of Mental Disorder, 5th Edition) which is an improvement of the DSM-IV. Another point of dereference could be the ICD-10, F60.8 by the

World Health Organization. Most professionals make use of the DSM-5 when making a diagnosis on narcissism, looking for a majority of similarity in the symptoms.

Obviously, diagnosis is done through a structured conversation, asking pointed questions with the person of interest. Other diagnostic methods such as blood tests and physical exams do not work in this case since narcissism has no physical symptoms. It is important to note that a large percentage of people with NPD rarely get treatment or seek professional help. For diagnostic purposes, having two or three of the NPD symptoms is not sufficient to label someone as a narcissist. Ideally, you should have five or more of the signs before a confirmed diagnosis are made.

Famous People Suspected with NPD

It would be unfair to say the narcissists only have a grandiose sense of self but unable to do anything that matches how they perceive themselves to be. Some narcissists have managed to stand out during the course of history as they showcase some talents, skills, and characteristics that might be rooted from their narcissistic personality disorder.

Of course, many narcissists have also marked history not as remarkable individuals but rather, people to be feared and to be kept away from society. In this chapter, you'll meet different people who have been diagnosed with NPD. Note though that some of the people in the list aren't purely NPD patients. Some of them are also diagnosed as being sociopaths and psychopaths, making their personalities even more complicated.

Paris Hilton

Although not exactly diagnosed as having NPD, it isn't surprising that many people theorize Parish Hilton as a narcissist. Her public actions certainly show her as having very little empathy for others. She is very self-loving and seems to be obsessed with self-image. Basically popular for being popular, Paris Hilton has always indicated that she loves the attention her presence generates. So, is this NPD behavior or is she simply reacting because of the obvious luxury she was raised in? It would be hard to tell without a full professional consultation.

Adolf Hitler

As already discussed, Adolf Hitler is a strong narcissist who has pushed boundaries during his time. Also described as a sociopath, Adolf Hitler is a great believer of his vision and has the charm to go with his goal of leading Germany. He showed signs and symptoms of NPD, including a grandiose sense of self-worth, always believing himself to be correct, lack of empathy, and more. He saw himself as above others, capable of uniting all people under his rule. His lack of empathy for basic human life led to millions of death, exterminating rivals, family members, and anyone who doesn't fit his prescribed views of what is right. He had a "grand plan" and the charm managed to help him get what he want but ultimately, Hitler's overestimation of his military power led to defeat.

Saddam Hussein

Saddam Hussein is comparable to Hitler in that they both held dangerous amounts of power. Perhaps it was this power that fueled their grandiose sense of self, formulating a plan to create a system that matched their ideals. Like Adolf Hitler, Saddam Hussein had no problems committing mass murder in favor of his goals. Like the malicious narcissist, Hussein was vindictive and made sure that his rivals know of his displeasure in the worst ways possible.

Do you want to find out more about narcissists? Check out the following movies!

- Gaslight

- Harold and Maude

- Grey Gardens

- September

- Gone with the Wind

- East of Eden

- The Devil Wears Prada

Chapter 2: Narcissism Types, Treatments and More

Types of Narcissist

In DSM V and ICD-10, NPD is essentially a single disorder with no marked subtypes. American psychologist Theodore Millon begs to differ however and have introduced five distinct subtypes when it comes to Narcissistic Personality Disorder:

- Compensatory Narcissist – people who have gone through extreme feelings of inferiority and wants to diminish the feeling by fantasizing about grandeur

- Unprincipled Narcissist – said to lack conscience and tends to be vengeful. They are often deceptive with no moral compass and exploitive of other people's weaknesses

- Elitist Narcissist – believes himself to be special or unique. Seeks recognition and often associates with people of power an achievement.

- Amorous Narcissist – hedonist and pursues sexual achievements and desires. Prone to lying and avoids intimacy of an emotional level.

- Fanatic Narcissist – much like Compensatory Narcissist except the feelings of shame and inferiority have started as early as childhood. They are trying to rebuild lost esteem by holding on to fantasies of greatness.

Treatment for Narcissism

Narcissists rarely see themselves as having problems, which is why very few actually seek treatment. In most cases, people with NPD only go to doctors after persistent requests by friends and families. The most common treatments often prescribe for NPD patients include:

- Individual Psychotherapy

- Group Therapy – a group therapy often involves close friends and family of the patient. A specialized psychotherapist often handles the flow of the conversation, guiding the topics to the aid the people involved.

- Specialized Environment

In some cases, a person with NPD is treated using a combination of the different approaches above. The decision is ultimately dependent on the psychotherapist handling the case because NPD patients respond differently to situations. For example, narcissist who displays lack of empathy might not do too well in Group Therapies but respond to Individual Psychotherapy.

Some medications have been prescribed for NPD but their success rate is disappointingly low. According to statistics, psychotherapy offers better performance rates in addressing narcissistic barriers through targeted approaches.

Narcissism and Criminal Tendencies

The term "narcissist" has such a negative connotation that people labeled with NPD are automatically thought to be social deviants. Note though that criminal tendencies are often associated with one specific NPD symptom: lack of empathy. Therefore, a person who does not have NPD (2 of 9 symptoms) and lacks empathy is more likely to cross moral barriers. An NPD patient (5 of 9 symptoms) who experiences empathy may be less inclined towards criminal tendencies.

It would be hard to deny however that people with NPD are more than capable of executing crime. In fact, many narcissistic turn into bullies, especially when they occupy a position of power. Although not necessarily executing crime, people with NPD may relish chipping away at a person's emotional health persistently, most often on people who occupy a lower position than them.

Malignant Self Love author Sam Vaknin, identifies narcissist as having "X-Ray Vision". They are capable of looking at someone and instantaneously locate their weak spots, often making use of this knowledge – possibly for their own ends. He further elaborates that people with NPD rarely feel bad about what they do – because they don't feel responsible for what has happened as a result of their actions.

Dealing with a Narcissist

A documentary reveals that narcissists are extremely hard to find – but what if you actually meet one? According to *Malignant Self Love*, the best way to cope with a narcissist is abandonment or the threat of such. People with NPD tend to distance themselves from emotional involvement – hence the use of humiliation and aggression when dealing with other people. In doing so, the narcissistic personality may trigger abandonment from their peers **BUT,** since they're the one who initiated the aggression/humiliation, they are able to tell themselves that it was expected. That THEY are the ones in control of the situation.

So what do you do when a narcissist tries their best to cause shame, anger or humiliation? You act as a mirror and perform exactly the same thing – prompting them into a sense of fear that might well be foreign to them. This is something that the narcissist personality is not prepared for, thus putting him into a calmly confused state.

Narcissists in Everyday Life

So if not all narcissist are criminals, then when are they most often seen? People with NPD can be found in all sorts of jobs, but mostly seen in the business sector. The very characteristics that identify them as NPD are often ruthlessly used to obtain achievements, therefore placing them in a position of power or upper management. Michael Maccoby, a leadership scholar introduces the term "productive narcissist", citing billionaire Bill Gates as one of them. He further expands that the secret to the success of these "productive narcissistic" is the presence of a sidekick or right hand man who keeps the negative aspects of NPD at bay. With these people providing "limitations", the narcissist becomes productive rather than destructive.

It is also said that many successful leaders are narcissist including Adolf Hitler and Joseph Stalin. However, author Sam Vaknin reveals that there is one situation that a narcissist finds to be the perfect grounds for their own personal desires and that is religion, specifically becoming a cult leader.

In a *Narcissists Documentary* also featuring Sam Vaknin, the title of cult leader is depicted to be the NPD's "wet dream". As a cult leader, narcissists are seen to be a representation of God themselves, therefore creating an abundance of adoration and praises all directed at them. The fact that cults are essentially a religion also means that narcissists working as cult leaders are in the position to create laws and guidelines with zero criticisms from their cult members. Simply put, this offers them absolute power over a group of people – something the narcissistic mind would be unable to resist.

Are you Dating a Narcissist?

If you think you're in a relationship with a narcissist, then there are some signs that should help you figure it out. Note though that unless you're a fully-trained professional therapist, your diagnosis may not be fully accurate.

- Does s/he think you're extremely lucky to be dating him/her?

- Does s/he talk about his many successes often and dismiss yours?

- Does s/he claim your achievements for his own?

- Does s/he want to be constantly flattered?

- Does s/he act like no one else "gets" him?

Case Study: David Berg

David Berg is the founder of the *Children of God*, is considered to be a narcissist, meeting more than 5 of the DSM-5 signs of DNP. He gave himself other names include "Moses David" and "King David", both of which were apparently derived from the Bible. During his leadership in the cult, Berg managed to collect thousands of followers, all believing him to be the mouth of God.

Streaks of Berg's narcissism have been witnessed firsthand by many, especially those who have been born into religion. In his more than 3,000 letters, Berg is very critical of "evil", and includes pedophilia laws (Berg is a rumored pedophile), Jews, capitalism and mainstream churches within those definitions.

Berg's desire for power and distinction can also be noted in his predictions of being the only one capable of comprehending the prophecies. He dubbed himself "the last prophet" before the end of the world, even going as far as predicting when the "end" would occur.

One of the most notable deviances of Berg is his propensity for promiscuity, often involving himself in sexual practices well above the norm. In fact, his narcissistic tendency for exploitation went so far as to the creation of a new bible that he wrote himself. Most of this contains information in support of promiscuity with Berg even lowering the age limit for sex and children taught as early as 6 to 7 years of age.

This is supported by the many books written by individuals who were born and grew up as members of the Children of God. The most popular of these published works is *Not*

Without my Sister, written by Kristina Jones and Celeste Jones.

Despite the many amoral acts that are connected with David Berg's name however, it is important to note that he only met 7 of the 9 characteristics of a person with Narcissistic Personality Disorder. The question arises though: what would an NPD with all 9 characteristics be like?

Chapter 3: Narcissists with People

Considering how narcissists rarely see themselves as having Narcissistic Personality Disorder, it's very rare for them to walk through the doctor's office and claim they have a problem. Their unique approach at things, however, usually means that everything around them is impacted by their values, behaviors, and beliefs. You'll find that although narcissists do not believe themselves to be such, a clear imprint of their self-love can be viewed through the people they socialize with on a daily basis.

Narcissists with People

When confronting narcissists, you'll find that they are fond of some behaviors that are markedly different from others. Through careful observation, you'll notice that these behaviors become more and more obvious, prompting you to make an unofficial diagnosis. Here are just some of the things that people with NPD often do when confronted in different situations:

Shift the Blame – narcissists never see a problem as their fault, rather it's YOUR fault for being vulnerable to the problem. For example, if they've hurt your feelings, then you are to blame for being so easily affected. Due to their grandiose view of themselves, narcissists do not perceive themselves as making mistakes. This view of self-perfection means that if they are not at fault, then logic dictates that someone else slipped up. Even when confronted with this idea, NPD patients are likely to cling to their self-image and deny any of the allegations. What's more, they can be quite strong with their denials while pointing the finger at someone else.

Condescending – the thing about narcissists is that *no one* is their equal. If even a single thing about a specific person is *unlike* them, this automatically puts them in a lower position. Hence, even if you and a narcissist graduated from the same university, your field of study may be a cause for contempt. If you happen to be in the same field of study, then they will simply focus on something else. Your job, background, religious beliefs, hobbies are all subjected to a narcissistic comparison with their own and nothing is ever good enough.

Two Personalities – funnily enough, narcissists are capable of hiding the fact that they consider other people beneath their notice. Some people who are acquainted with narcissists believe that the person is one of the nicest people they have ever met. With other people however, narcissists may switch on their more cruel side, preferring to act condescending and insulting. A narcissist may turn on the charm for a variety of reasons. First, they may do so when meeting someone for the first time. They might want to impress this person or the brief meeting is not enough for the narcissist to show his true colors. In the work area, NPD patients may choose to show their "charm" to higher ranking employees while being insulting to anyone of higher rank.

Pursuit of Revenge – vindictiveness is a common trait for many narcissists. In fact, they don't stop after getting even but remain spiteful for as long as it can be done. The emotion is usually triggered if you try to question what they're doing or indicate/imply that they've done something incorrectly. Since they believe themselves to be infallible, any implication of errors made towards them is taken seriously. Some narcissists with no proper control over their emotions may become spiteful, continuing to insult or be malicious to someone to no end. Unfortunately, narcissists make very bad enemies because they are capable of homing in on a person's "weak spot" and targeting this to no end. As mentioned by an expert, they possess "x-ray" vision which makes them more capable of giving harsh punishment in retaliation.

They're Mirrors – an interesting question put out by most people is: *are narcissists aware of what they're doing*? The simple answer is yes. In fact, people with NPD go so far as accuse others of doing what they have done. No mistake about it – narcissists are aware of the lines of morality and can easily tell between right and wrong. This is why whenever they do something wrong, they do their best to hide the fact. In most cases, this is done by acting like a mirror. For example, if the narcissist is plotting against you, then you'll find yourself being accused of nefarious planning against the narcissist. If this person just lied to you, then you will be accused of lying.

Complications of Narcissism

People with NPD often struggle with their condition as much as the people they deal with on a daily basis. Studies have revealed that when left untreated, narcissists can spiral into complications that could worsen their present position. Following are some of the most common complications that follow NPD:

- Suicidal thoughts

- Self harming

- Alcohol abuse

- Substance abuse

- Depression

- Problems with school, work, friends, and family

NPD patients may also suffer from different mental disorders including: *mood disorders, paranoia, and anorexia nervosa.*

The Narcissist View on Morality

As already mentioned earlier, narcissist can distinguish perfectly well between right and wrong. When asked upfront about the rightness/wrongness of committing theft, they will give the morally-accepted answer. *So why do they still do wrong things if they know it's wrong?* The catch here is that although they understand the wrongness of the situation, a narcissist cannot empathize with the victim. Most people can put themselves in the victim's place and therefore get a glimmer of the pain that someone else is going through. This is not something that someone with NPD can do. Regardless of the nature of the "problem", it is always the other person's fault and it will never happen to them.

Chapter 4: Narcissists in the Family

What happens to husbands, wives, or children if one person in the family is a narcissist? It can be tough to live with someone with NPD. Since NPDs are very comfortable in their own homes, it is highly unlikely for them to bring on the charm when dealing with family members. Hence, if you're living with someone who has NPD, rest assured that you'll be able to notice some symptoms or a general tendency towards mood problems. This chapter will talk about what it's like to have a narcissist parent:

Narcissist Parent

The core characteristics of a narcissist make them very bad parents. Oddly enough, this doesn't usually mean that they ignore their child or neglect them. Doctors theorize that people with NPD have a very low self esteem – to the point where they have to build it up by putting down others. The child therefore, is a source of confidence. The dependency of the child to them as a parent gives them power and puts them in the position of being infallible. After all, parents are supposed to be the child's guide and source of support during his growing-up years.

Unfortunately, the narcissistic parent takes this one step further by becoming more obsessive with their children. While some moms/dads relish the growing independence of their children, narcissistic parents are more likely to resent and become envious of their child's widening horizons.

As a child grows up, the narcissistic parent may regard him/her as a puppet, existing solely for the needs of the mother/father. The child is there for the benefit of the parent, often limiting their exposure to the outside world. A narcissistic parent may become controlling, possessive, and demand attention. In *Children of the Self Absorbed*, a book written by Nina W. Brown, she also notes that narcissistic parents tend to: *refuse to listen to their children, do not communicate emotionally with the child, make insulting comments about their offspring, use the items of their children without asking,* and more.

Signs of a Narcissistic Parent

Do you think you have a narcissistic parent? Look back and try to review the actions of your mom/dad while growing up. Some clear indicators of NPD in parents include, but are not limited to, the following:

- Claims the successes of their child. They might say that a specific talent came from them and they've generously passed on to the child.

- Incredibly dictatorial, as narcissistic parents like to tell their children what to do or how to act in almost every situation. They also prefer to make decisions for the child.

- Parents with NPD usually have a hard time empathizing with their children. They can also be quite adept in emotional blackmail.

Growing Up for Kids with Narcissistic Parents – unfortunately, being raised by a narcissist parent means that the child will suffer through some emotional abuses before reaching his/her teenage years. In fact, kids of narcissists tend to become narcissists themselves or start to suffer from codependency.

Throughout growing up, children of narcissists are viewed as merely "extensions" of their parents. Therefore, their unique characteristics are obliterated in favor of the parent's personal motives. Many of these children are exposed to a "good-bad" cycle wherein the parent shows them the good side of their nature. However, if the child fails to perform to the parent's expectations, they will be forced to endure "punishment", whether it is physical or psychological in nature. A good example of narcissistic parenting is mother/father who pushes their child to become a lawyer, usually to meet their own goals rather than for the betterment of the child. Worse, some narcissists may make it seem as though they are pushing the child hard as a favor to the child. If the expectations are not met, the parent will have no problem cutting off the child from his/her life.

Types of Narcissistic Parents

There are basically two ways a narcissist will approach parenthood. Depending on which type a mother/father falls in, the child may become another NPD personality or someone with codependency issues. That being said, following are the three different types known today:

- *Ignoring Parents* – these are parents who remain true to the "self-love" core of the narcissistic personality. They do not see their children as important and therefore dismiss them entirely, often ignoring some of the child's successes when it comes to friends and school. The Ignoring Parent often puts a boundary between themselves and the child, leading to a lack of love and care in the relationship. Unfortunately, this doesn't mean that the child is safe from derogatory comments coming from a narcissistic parent. You'll find that for people with NPD, castigating a child for his/her mistakes is easy but giving praise is often not done.

- *Engulfing Parents* – this is the opposite side of the spectrum wherein parents do no ignore their child, but smother them with care and attention. Unfortunately, this is not the healthy attention that usually comes from parents. The engulfing mother/father usually sees the child as an extension of him/herself. Although this works out for babies and toddlers, the continuing growth of the child becomes threatening for the parent. In most cases, narcissistic parents ignore the "lines" of privacy and become too encroached in their children's private lives. Good examples of this happening include reading the child's emails, phone messages, asking personal questions, and being too inquisitive about what should have been private topics.

Narcissistic Family Dynamics

NPD parents usually have predictable family dynamics, especially if there are two or more children. The kids usually fall within one of the two categories.

- *Golden Child* – this is the child that the parent sees as an "extension" of their personality. Hence, this particular child can do no wrong and is often praised and encouraged by the parent. S/he is also the one exposed to much control as the parent view the child's achievements as theirs. Hence, the golden child is often pushed and prodded towards success.

- *Scapegoat Child* – the Scapegoat Child is the one who is always wrong. Should there be any problems, the scapegoat child is the one to blame for it all. Anything the child achieves is ignored but all the mistakes are made glaringly obvious, severely damaging the child's self-esteem. Unfortunately, this kind of treatment on the child sets the tone for everyone else in the house. If the NPD parent has other children, chances are they will follow the parent's footsteps and also degrade the scapegoat child.

Others argue that there is a third type, dubbed as the Ignored Child. This is the child that the parent doesn't acknowledge at all, except from meeting his/her basic needs. However, others are of the opinion that the ignored child also falls within the category of the scapegoat child.

How It's Done – NPD Parent-Controlling Techniques

It's been mentioned time and again that NPD parents like to exert control over their children – but how exactly do they make this happen? Following are the different approaches NPD parents make to control their children:

- *Explicit Control* – this is the most obvious one and unfortunately, even non-narcissistic parents use this method so it's not a clear indicator. The simplest example of this would be telling the child to follow orders or risk punishment of any form.

- *Goal Oriented Control* - this is where NPD parents set up a goal and encourages their children to work with them in order to achieve said goal. However, an NPD parent is the one who sets the goal rather than the child. In truth, whatever goal that needs to be achieved is actually the *parent's* goal, with him/her using the child as a substitute.

- *Love Withdrawal Control* – this is characterized by the parent qualifying or labeling the love s/he offers. The idea is that the child is only deserving of the parent's love if s/he follows orders. If the child misbehaves or doesn't meet expectations, the love is immediately withdrawn.

- *Emotional Incest Control* - a common example of this is when a parent says: *You are the most important person in my life. You are the only person that I really love.* Now, this might sound normal for most but an NPD person pushes this to the extreme. They use the child as a substitute for unsatisfactory relationships with others. Note though that this doesn't necessarily mean fully-consummated incest.

- *Guilt-Driven Control* – this is usually characterized by the parent emphasizing something s/he has given up in favor of the child. The perceived sacrifice is brought out every time the child shows any chance of straying from the parent's wants.

- *Codependent Control* – in simple terms, this type of control emphasizes the parent's need for the child. The mother often underlines their need for the relationship, preventing the child from forging out in his own. Hence, he remains codependent on the parent until adulthood.

Narcissism in Life and Pop Culture - Not surprisingly, narcissism has been a source of interest for many, especially those in the medical profession. Understanding narcissism and how it affects people has long been the subject of many movies, some of which are specifically made with the narcissistic parent personality in mind. Following are some movies that are believed to showcase narcissism in parents. If you're still unsure of how this works, then try hunting out the movies listed below:

- *Mommie Dearest* – a chillingly accurate classic, Mommie Dearest is possibly one of the best movies about mother-daughter relations. In this case, the mother is a narcissist and holds a less than appealing relationship with her child.

- *Ever After – A Cinderella Story* – mostly a romance movie, this Drew Barrymore movie offers glimpses of a narcissistic mother in the form of the evil-stepmother. In a similar story to Cinderella, the mother raises two children – one of which grows up with the same narcissistic tendencies. The other daughter showcases other characteristics a child might develop when in the presence of a narcissistic parent: codependency.

- *Dead Poet's Society* - a classic, the movie portrays a narcissistic father with a child displaying the characteristics of someone who has lived with a self-loving individual. To make matters worse, the mother is an enabler who tends to bow to the stronger personality.

Chapter 5: Narcissism and Social Media

Here's an interesting topic worth discussing – the link of narcissism with social media, more specifically the "selfie" habit that seems to be sweeping practically anyone who is currently using the internet.

A popular website once published that taking "selfies" has been declared a mental disorder. Although this was later revealed as a hoax, there's no question that the statement bears studying. Are excessive selfies a sign of a mental disorder? Is this apparent electronic extreme-love for one's self a sign of Narcissistic Personality Disorder?

Studies on Selfies

Studies reveal that the social media actually helps feed the narcissistic personality. Although this alone may not be enough for a diagnosis, there's no question that self-love online can still be a destructive phase for many teenagers. In the book *The Narcissistic Epidemic: Living in the Age of Entitlement,* the authors note that since the 1980s, there have been more recorded cases of narcissism. That clearly defines all the "Millenials" who have been born after 1980. The possibility of higher NPD tendencies in the youth of today are further underlined by the *"Me, Me, Me Generation"* article in TIME Magazine.

One important thing to keep in mind is that narcissists are essentially insecure within their cores. Since they're not sure of themselves, they force their personalities on to other people to demonstrate their strengths. This trait, therefore, makes Facebook a very powerful tool for narcissists. It serves as a bulletin board of sorts that contains all updates in their life and what's more – other people can read these updates. Hence, the online narcissist further believes that everyone is interested in what he is doing.

To take it one step further, online narcissists are rarely honest with the things they post. In the same way people choose their prettiest pictures for their profiles, narcissists make a point of posting information that will put them in the best light. Other signs of online narcissism include, but are not limited to, the following:

- Almost daily changes of profile pictures

- Constantly checking your social media account for updates, changes, likes, retweets, or comments on your posts

- You like to post everything that comes through your mind, and every idea or conversation you've had with other people

- Excessively sharing what's happening in your life by posting pictures of even the most mundane things

- You have a large friends list, probably numbering more than 3,000 with still more being added everyday! Obviously, you do not know all these people but this doesn't bother the NPD personality in the slightest

- Being extremely eager when it comes to bragging about the smallest accomplishments in your life.

Whether it's a recent out-of-country trip or receiving candy from an officemate.

- If hanging out in social media websites make you feel better about yourself, then you might be dealing with a mild narcissistic problem

Chapter 6: Understanding Sociopaths and Psychopaths

Although there are marked differences between a sociopath and psychopath, the two terms are considered to be practically the same. To make this personality disorder easier to understand however, this chapter will be discussed by placing both psychopaths and sociopaths side by side with an attempt to highlight significant distinctions between the two.

Definition and Symptoms

DSM-IV defines a sociopath/psychopath as someone with an antisocial personality disorder who often has zero recognition of common moral standards. They are often defined as lacking in empathy, causing them to fake typical human emotions. Originally dubbed as "moral insanity" during the 1830s, the medical profession has managed to compile a fairly comprehensive profile for a sociopath/psychopath.

1. Charm - sociopaths/psychopaths have been known to exude charm if the need arises.

2. Exaggerated Sense of Self Importance – much like a narcissist, sociopaths/psychopaths tend to see themselves as unique compared to others. They often have big views of themselves and a grandiose view of their future

3. Lack of Empathy - sociopaths/psychopaths do not recognize human emotions such as shame, guilt, or

remorse. This makes them highly dangerous because there is no internal moral compass that guides them. Some people refer to sociopaths/psychopaths as "blank slates" because they also do not recognize happiness, joy and other positive emotions. However, they are capable of faking these emotions, often showing them as an effort to blend in the group.

4. Manipulative – thanks to their superficial charm, sociopaths/psychopaths are more than capable of manipulating people to meet their own needs.

5. Lying - sociopaths/psychopaths aren't just good liars but they're also very consistent with their lies. They are dubbed as "pathological liars" with an ability to be incredibly convincing. Some have been known to take lie detector tests and pass.

6. Seeks Excitement - sociopaths/psychopaths are easily bored which makes them seek higher sources of excitement. This is another factor that can make them dangerous as sociopaths/psychopaths are never satisfied. Deviance often starts early with pursuits of excitement ranging from social exploits, petty criminal activities, physical violence, verbal violence and more.

7. No Solid Life Plan – people with this personality disorder tend to move around a lot, often exploiting other people instead of creating solid plans for the future. They are more than capable of devising a new life, often changing their image to escape past problems with no difficulty.

Sociopaths/psychopaths are also noted for being highly

secretive with a touch of paranoia. Few psychopaths voluntarily seek treatment because – as with narcissists – they rarely see anything that is wrong with them.

Diagnosing a Psychopath or Sociopath

Diagnosing a psychopath/sociopath is often done by following the DSM-IV diagnostic criteria.

- The person has showcased repeated disregard for rules, regulations and the rights of others as ascertained by normal cultural standards. The said person has been doing these acts since the age of fifteen, usually involving one or more of the following: (1) acts that lead to capture by officers of the law, (2) marked impulsiveness, (3) swindling people either for profit or for fun, (4) disregard for other people's safety, (5) rationalizing any harm they cause to other people, (6) inability to honor obligations usually financial in nature, (7) poor behavior in the work setting, (8) instigates assault, (9) conduct disorders evident at the age of 15, and (10) the above signs cannot be attributed to any other mental disorder.

Psychotherapists are often reluctant in diagnosing someone as a psychopath, sociopath or even a narcissist if they haven't reached the age of 18. Therefore, the DSM-IV Diagnosis is only fully confirmed when the person of interest reaches the acceptable age and essentially adapts the characteristics he might carry through adulthood.

Childhood of Sociopaths/Psychopaths

Textbook sociopaths/psychopaths usually have the same childhood predilections, often involving the torture of animals and sexually deviant behaviors. Although doctors aren't keen in diagnosing personality disorders in young children, their childhood stories often involve great tragedies or events that essentially turned them into sociopaths/psychopaths. Dennis Radner known as the BTK Killer confessed to criminal tendencies even as a young child, often killing animals and stealing women underwear. Some signs of sociopathy such as overexcitement, impulsiveness, inability to plan ahead, charm and preference for isolation can also be noted in the childhood of diagnosed sociopaths/psychopaths. Of course, an accurate diagnosis for anyone under 18 is often difficult.

Causes for Psychopath/Sociopath

The exact reason why people become sociopaths/psychopaths is unknown despite the extensive study on the matter. Much like narcissism, it is believed that the condition comes down to two factors: nature and nurture.

- Genetic Link - DNA is often cited as a contributing factor in many healthy conditions, even psychopathy. The idea is having a family member with this condition heightens the chances of you having it as well. Studies have also theorized that there are hormonal factors that contribute to a person's psychopathy. High levels of testosterone (usually connected to aggression) combined with minimal amounts of serotonin and cortisol in the body are said to increase a person's predilection for the personality disorder.

- Environment – Many known sociopaths/psychopaths have experienced "turning points" in their lives which might have contributed to their personality disorders later in life. In Ted Bundy's case, it was learning about his true parentage followed by the breakup of a relationship. In John Wayne Gacy's case, it could be attributed to the childhood abuse he suffered from his fatter.

Treatment for Sociopaths/Psychopaths

Due to the basic characteristics displayed by sociopaths/psychopaths, there is no basic treatment for the personality disorder. The condition is addressed on a person-to-person basis in order to fully understand the most dominant characteristics and how to address them properly. In many cases however, the first thing therapists have to tackle is forming a bond with the patient. Due to their lack of empathy, it is crucial for doctors to first establish trust between sociopaths/psychopaths and the person delivering the treatment. Not being able to succeed in this first basic step can halt the treatment process completely.

Essentially, therapists would be rehabilitating sociopaths/psychopaths and teaching them the skills they lack in society. This often involves helping them develop empathy, improving social skills, psychotherapy, behavior therapy and more. Medications may be prescribed but they are only used to handle the symptoms without curing the problem itself.

Case Study: Dennis Radner

Known as the BTK Killer which stands for *Bind, Torture and Kill*, Dennis Radner is a prime example for sociopaths/psychopaths. In his career as a criminal, he killed a total of 10 women and has stalked others with the intent to kill. Although Radner's list is considerably shorter than other serial killers, it is his obvious lack of remorse that really registers among the public. In fact, Radner's retelling of his crimes during the trial lacked emotion and were told in a markedly flat tone of voice. In his retelling, Radner has even given his killer alter-ego a name, referring to it in the 2nd person.

What is even more surprising is Radner's incredible ability to blend in society. Married for 34 years, Radner was elected president of his church and was even a Cub Scout leader. Needless to say, his involvement in the BTK killings were completely unsuspected by everyone around him.

The constant need for excitement and stimulation is also evident in Radner's love for corresponding with the police. He is known for sending many letters to the officers of law, often taunting them of the fact that they are unable to catch him.

Chapter 7: Psychopathy versus Sociopathy, Is There a Difference?

If you'll notice, the definition for sociopath and psychopath are practically the same. In some instances, there is no clear line separating the two, leading many people to use the terms interchangeably. Extensive studies about the personality disorder however have turned up marked differences between the two conditions.

Sociopathy and psychopathy are often used interchangeably. These two terms are used to describe people who lack conscience and act without any regard to others. People affected by these disorders are often thought of as hopeless cases and therefore doomed for life. The DSM definition even puts both personality disorders under one roof, antisocial personality disorder. While it is true these two have plenty of similarities, they also have characteristics that are distinct to both. And those differences include the following.

Nature versus Nurture

DSM-IV determines the most apparent similarity between pychopaths and sociopaths. That is they share anti social behavior. But behind this commonality is a major difference that sets one apart from the other. Such is the cause of these personality disorders.

Recent studies reveal that psychopaths are born while sociopaths are made. This means that psychopaths tend to have a genetic link (nature) while the sociopaths often encounter life events (nurture) that alters their personality.

The debate between nature and nurture as causes of personality disorders is an age old one. Most scholars decide to be in the middle stating that both biological and environmental factors have an important if not equal role in shaping every individual.

There is still an ongoing debate about the causes. A lot of experts believe that both nurture and nature factors are involved in their development. But plenty of scholars seem to be more open to the idea that while sociopathy comes as a result of a person's upbringing or environmental factors; psychopathy is a result of nature. In other words, pyschopathy is believed to stem from hereditary and genetic factors.

A psychopath is born that way. This individual will always be a psychopath. The disorder is deeply rooted in this person's chemical makeup. Usually, psychopathy symptoms show at a very young age. There are signs that tell something is wrong or is not right with the individual.

Studies show that the brain waves of a psychopath are quite different not only from the rest of the population but also distinct to a sociopath. A psychopath's brain responds distinctively to certain stimuli.

They do not possess the neurological framework to be able to have morality or a sense of ethics. Psychopathy is seen as a physiological defect which leads to the underdevelopment of the area of the brain which is responsible for emotions and impulse control. Their genetic makeup is responsible for the way they lack emotions, their lack of concern towards others and their reaction to fear. Their brains are wired differently. And it is not something that can be rewired or reboot.

In other words, psychopaths did not choose to be that way. It is something that they cannot help. And the most unfortunate thing is they do not think there is anything wrong with what they do. At least they don't feel there is something wrong simply because they cannot think the way we do.

On the other hand, sociopathy is believed to come as a result of environmental factors. A person's upbringing has a huge impact on how he or she behaves, acts and thinks. While a child may be born a psychopath, a sociopath is born like the rest of us, normal.

There is nothing wrong with their brain waves. Theirs are wired like the rest of ours. However, due to upbringing and environmental factors, they change. They learn to become sociopaths. And the more they are exposed to violence, abuse and neglectful parents, the more they come closer to becoming a sociopath.

Differences in Temperament

When it comes to enforcing control over their actions, sociopaths are more impulsive compared to psychopaths. The latter tends to plan before pursuing an activity while sociopaths are more impulsive, deciding to take action on a whim.

In general, sociopaths often have a good understanding proper social behavior. It is usually easy for them to blend in. In fact, they can be fully functional in society. Most of them are not temperamental in nature as well. The sociopath's problem is not innate. It is just a result of long term and early exposure to bad environment or bad company, negligence, violence and abuse among others.

The psychopaths are different in that they lack the capacity to understand social norms. However, they are able to cope with what is socially expected of them if only on the surface. What makes them different from sociopaths is their fearlessness and impulsiveness. These traits push them to take risks. They are described to be intellectually superior too and they use such to their advantage.

A psychopath's temperamental nature will drive this person to take risks, even unnecessary ones. And they are less likely to have control over their temperament and the issues that come with it simply because it is innate. They are born with temperamental issues.

On the surface, a psychopath may appear charismatic, gentle mannered and well spoken. But behind that mask is a callous and cold hearted individual. In other words, a psychopath goes through a complete disguise.

A sociopath on the other hand, also usually relates to people with charm. But instead of hiding from a completely different persona, the sociopath does let some part of his real self come through. This person may be disorganized and he or she can be easily annoyed too. A sociopath may speak abruptly and often this individual is quick to show temper. Despite such temperament, between the two, the sociopath is much less likely to kill.

Feel Guilty or Not Guilty

According to DSM-IV, both psychopaths and sociopaths lack empathy. In other words, they are incapable of feeling guilt. But there is a good reason to believe such definition is inconclusive.

Because psychopaths lack moral code of ethics, they are unfamiliar with feeling empathy and remorse. In which case, they have a tendency to manipulate other people. They will lie all the way to reach their goal. They live a parasitic lifestyle. And they are expected to live on in violation of societal norms. All the time they are doing others wrong, they feel nothing, not even an inch of guilt.

Sociopaths on the other hand, are capable of feeling guilt for their actions. However, it is reserved for people they have an emotional connection with. They feel remorse when they realize they have hurt those who are close to them, those they were able to build a relationship with. With regard to people outside their circle however, they will behave like a psychopath. That is they do not accept social norms.

Another difference is that unlike psychopaths, sociopaths have a lesser tendency to lie or become manipulative at least not to their families or other people they are associated with. As a matter of fact, they can have genuine feelings for people within their circle.

For a psychopath, everyone is just the same, whether you belong to the inner circle or not. In fact, a psychopath does not have an inner circle. Everyone is just a means to an end, family, friend, life partner or not. They simply cannot make the distinction.

Building Social Relations

Both psychopaths and sociopaths suffer from antisocial personality disorder which means they tend to steer clear of social situations. The difference however is that psychopaths are incapable of sustaining a relationship. On the other hand, sociopaths are highly capable of maintaining relationships, often collecting a large set of friends.

It can prove difficult to spot a psychopath because they blend in so well you would not be able to guess there is something wrong unless you have been with them for quite some time, long enough to recognize the signs.

For a psychopath, it is not difficult to blend in to society. While they may be incapable of feeling true emotions, they are quite capable of mimicking sentiments and make it appear as if such feelings are genuine. They can charm their way into the hearts of potential partners. They are also well organized.

For a sociopath, maintaining a relationship is not a problem. But their relationships are most likely parasitic by nature. They are heavily dependent on other people.

Psychopaths face a lot of difficulty with their relationships. Their deficiencies make it much tougher for them to build new relationships. In fact, they also have troubles maintaining their existing relationships even with their family. Usually, they live by themselves and they prefer it that way.

Career Chances

When it comes to career life, psychopaths do better than sociopaths. Plenty of psychopaths are successful in their chosen fields. They have the ability to charm and adjust so they can make themselves likeable. This way, other people can easily interact with them. They have a good understanding of how normal people operate and the emotions they feel. This knowledge allows them to easily manipulate people.

The career lives of sociopaths are not as fruitful as that of the psychopaths. They get bored easily. They are less likely to stick to a job and this makes it always impossible for them to build a career.

Dealing with Boredom

People suffering from psychopathy or sociopathy have issues with boredom. Everyone gets bored but psychopaths and sociopaths are different in that they are not capable of containing their boredom. To respond to boredom, sociopaths are more likely to create drama or stir conflict. They would seek attention from people around them. And you can expect them to do whatever it takes to get the attention they wanted.

On the other hand, psychopaths are more capable of channeling their boredom. Instead of creating drama or stirring conflict among their peers, they would find something constructive to do in order to relieve their boredom. These people are considered to be highly intelligent and creative.

Violent Tendencies

Since they have a higher predisposition to violence, psychopaths are more likely to be involved in a physical crime. Their criminal tendencies veer towards impulsiveness, often driven by an "in the moment" attitude.

On the other hand, sociopaths take minimal risks. Their goals are often to make sure that exposure is very unlikely compared to psychopaths who rarely consider the risks involved because they are fearless by nature. Psychopaths have a higher tendency towards violence than sociopaths.

More often than not, unsuspecting strangers prefer to be in the company of a psychopath and deem sociopaths as threatening. The truth is the former is much more fearful. You have more reason to be afraid of a psychopath. While both have violent tendencies, a psychopath's tendency to kill is much stronger.

Both sociopaths and psychopaths have violent tendencies. Even normal people have a tendency to commit illegal acts. But what psychopaths and sociopaths are capable of may be unimaginable for the normal person. Their nature makes them well capable of committing the most heinous crimes.

Although it is wrong to conclude that everyone affected with these personality disorders are criminals or murderers, what you need to understand is that these people do not think and act like normal people do. An act which may be unthinkable to you is something exciting for these individuals.

If a psychopath is to commit a crime, he or she will be well organized. Such will make it difficult for him or her to get caught. With the psychopath's ability to mimic emotions and the charismatic personality, he or she may not even make it to the list of suspects. This individual is physical and emotional control is outstanding.

This person does not feel fear. He or she is capable of maintaining composure even in a horrifying situation. It does not mean the psychopath does not recognize that what he or she does is wrong. It's just that this person could not care less.

Like a psychopath, the sociopath also possesses violent tendencies. The difference is that sociopaths are much less organized. Unlike psychopaths who can show composure in the most terrifying situations, sociopaths have a tendency to become easily agitated. They also get easily nervous and may appear ill tempered.

Psychopaths are one step ahead of sociopaths in that they plan everything up to the smallest of details. Sociopaths however, are likely to act spontaneously. They have no regard of consequences.

As compared to psychopaths, sociopaths will find it much more difficult to commit heinous crimes. And that is for the simple reason that they are capable of feeling attachment at least to their loved ones. They may lie, manipulate and hurt other people but they are less likely to harm those they genuinely care about. When they do, they feel guilt creeping in.

To make this easier for you, this chart offers an overview of the psychopath/sociopath qualities and their marked differences.

	Psychopath	Sociopath
Social Relationships	Efficient in blending in social situations Relationships are tough Their relationships are parasitic by nature	Have an understanding of social norms Capable of building and sustaining relationships
Career	Often successful in their chosen professions	Incapable of holding steady employment
Violence and Crime	Varies in violent tendencies, often engaging in well-planned crimes with little risks to themselves	Highly violent, often involved in opportunistic crimes with little thoughts to the risks involved
Behavior	Highly controlled	Unpredictable

It is important to note that despite all the attention being focused on these personality disorder, there are still some unknown fields of sociopathy and psychopathy.

Chapter 8: Deeper Look at Psychopaths

Psychopath

Some articles on sociopath versus psychopath identify the latter as the more "dangerous" of two. Essentially, psychopaths are defined as a severe mental disorder involving violent behavior and antisocial tendencies. Their most defining characteristic is the inability to feel shame, guilt and various other emotions. Serial killers like Ted Bundy and TBK are often identified as psychopaths although they exhibit more of the characteristics of sociopaths. In many cases, the terms psychopath and sociopath are interchangeable when it comes to identifying serial killers.

Relationship Cycle

Not all psychopaths become the bane of social environment. Others have successfully managed to tamp down their inclinations and blend in with the normal lifestyle. As already mentioned, a sociopath need not be a criminal. Considering their unique personality however, how exactly does a psychopath act when it comes to relationships?

Psychopaths follow a predictable pattern when it comes to relationships, as determined by experts. Some call it the "psychopathic bond" while others simply label it as emotional rape. The process usually goes like this: *idealize, devalue, and discard.*

- *Idealize* – at this stage, the psychopath still sees you as an object of desire and great excitement. The psychopath will pay very close attention to you in order to find out your greatest wants, desires, and weaknesses. Most people who enter relationships with a psychopath would feel incredibly lucky during this stage – believing that they've finally found their perfect partner.

- *Devalue* – due to their inability to empathize and since they feel strong bursts of emotions, psychopaths usually become bored very quickly. When the psychopath feels as though s/he knows everything s/he wishes to know, this is when the second stage begins. S/he will start to move away from you emotionally, withdrawing any support he might have provided before. The psychopath's treatment of you will become worse, but s/he will also offer just enough encouragement to keep you in the relationship. According to a psychopath's partner, the *"devalue"* stage is when psychopaths start testing their mate, seeing how badly they can be treated before they bail out.

- *Discard* – at some point, even the Devalue stage becomes boring for the psychopath, causing them to leave their partner entirely.

How Do You Know You Are Dating a Psychopath?

Male versus Female Psychopaths

When we are talking about core personalities, male and female psychopaths have many similarities. Both men and women affected by this personality disorder are deceptive and self centered who have shallow emotions and completely lack empathy. They tend to manipulate and exploit other people and feel no remorse. They deceive and use others for self serving reasons. Psychopathic men and women often blame other people when they are caught up with the consequences of their actions.

Male and female psychopaths use physical appearance and charm for manipulation. Women, however, are more likely to use sex as well as outright violence to meet their ends. While there are many similarities between a male and female psychopath, there are also notable differences.

Male psychopaths are twice as common as female psychopaths. Psychopathic women are more likely to resort to a different strategy to fulfill their needs. This may come as a result of gender role expectations. As compared to male psychopaths, women do not usually engage in physical threats and animal cruelty. Rather, they use verbal manipulation and flirting. Psychopathic women are also more likely to victimize their own children.

Psychopaths as Parents

It's usually never a good thing for psychopaths to be parents. Despite the genetic link, there is no emotional bliss that comes forth with the birth of the child – both for the psychopath mother and father. In typical psychopath fashion, they do not see the child as a person but rather a possession – like the television or the car. Hence, the need to help develop the child's personality and help him through his growing up years is non-existent. At best, a psychopathic parent will ignore the child. At worst, the parent may become abusive – both mentally and physically, in some cases even sexually.

Psychopathy is genetic. This means a child with either a psychopathic father or mother has a predisposition to develop the disorder. But this does not mean children of psychopathic parents automatically are psychopaths too. A child may or may not inherit the genes. If the mother is the psychopath in the family, there is a greater chance of inheriting the genes. But if the father is the psychopath, it is less likely.

It is important to understand that anti personality disorders like psychopathy can come from both biological and environmental factors. While the child may not get the genes of his or her psychopathic parents, being exposed to the nurturing tactics or lack thereof of his or her personality disordered parent/s does have a huge effect. At the same time, it is possible for a child of psychopathic parents to grow up normally. Attentive parenting can, in fact, help mitigate and even prevent the development of psychopathy in the child. It is important for the child to learn and experience real love, genuine empathy and impulse control.

Psychopaths are probably the worst and most terrible parents. For one, they do not know empathy, love and impulse control so they are incapable of teaching their children such things. In fact, they will not even bother with it.

Psychopathic parents do not feel love for their children. They do not have any concern about their child's welfare. They do not care if their child grows up healthy and whether or not their child becomes a productive member of society in the future. A psychopath does not see his or her child as an individual. Rather, psychopathic parents treat their children as mere possessions. They treat their own children like they would a car and other possessions.

When other people are watching, the psychopathic parent may act as if he or she is an excellent parent. It is also likely for this parent to show martyrdom. To an outsider, he or she may be well admired for the sacrifices he or she is making for his or her kids. When no one is looking, however, the psychopathic parent shows no affection and no genuine interest in caring for the child.

As mentioned previously, the psychopathic parent sees the child as nothing more than a personal possession. To the psychopath, his or her child exists to meet his or her needs. Affection may be showed but only when the child does things that feed the parent's ego.

When the child shows rebellion or resistance, the psychopathic parent feels betrayed and such behavior is dealt with through punishment and harsh criticism in an effort to bring the child back on line. The psychopathic parent feels the inherent need to mold his or her child the way who he or she wants the child to be. This is why this parent cannot allow his or her kid to grow up normally.

In some cases, psychopaths will abandon or neglect their children. In other cases, they abuse them. However, rarely will a psychopath parent engage in physical abuse. Instead, they usually abuse their children emotionally or psychologically. They lie to their kids. They would constantly break their promises. Often, they would keep changing the rules. This can be very confusing to the child. In fact, it causes a distortion of the kid's sense of reality.

Even if a child does not inherit the genes, growing up in an unstable environment, the child is likely to develop other psychological issues. Such may include depression and anxiety. These children often do not have any clue about what a healthy relationship is like. They do not know how it is to be in a healthy family. It is more likely that they would grow up involved with other personality disordered individuals like the people they grew up with. That's what is normal to them.

Unfortunately, this abusive cycle at home can take its toll on the children of psychopaths. Although some of them turn out well, many grow up to develop other personality disorders including narcissism and codependency. The well-known psychopath Ed Gein, who killed and desecrated corpses, is said to have an antisocial mother who may also be a borderline psychopath.

To be truly normal, these kids need to do internal untangling. They need to heal and deal with the deep emotional pain their psychopath parents have caused them. And such can happen through formal counseling.

Psychopaths in History

Edward Gein – Edward Theodore Gein was convicted of killing Bernice Worde and desecrating the graves of many other in his crazed pursuit of his mother. Definitely a mother's boy, Gein grew up with mostly his mother for company and seemed to tip over the edge when she finally died, leaving him all alone. He first started digging up corpses of women he believed looks like his mother and started cutting up their parts to be used in the house.

In his trial, Gein was believed to be mentally imbalanced. This is the marked difference between the sociopath and the psychopath. While sociopath Ted Bundy is able to easily blend in and appear normal, psychopath Ed Gein was seen as a little "off". Both weren't originally viewed as dangerous but Gein was less capable of functioning in society.

Chapter 9: Deeper Look at Sociopaths

Sociopath

The simplest way to define a sociopath is someone who suffers from a personality disorder characterized by antisocial tendencies with no moral compass. A lack of conscience is often one of the most common descriptions used for this personality disorder. Known sociopaths include Ted Bundy, Jeffrey Dahmer, and Charles Manson.

Sociopaths in Relationships

There's really no large difference between the psychopathic and sociopathic relationship cycle. Sociopaths also naturally follow the "Idealize, Devalue, Discard" system when it comes to partnerships and relationships. Of course, they might do this with a little more panache, capable of using their charm. According to some dating gurus, there are several ways of spotting a sociopath in the event that you think you're dating one:

- Having very few friends, s/he might not introduce you to anyone in his/her life – not even family. In fact, a sociopath may not even talk about family.

- Incredibly attentive – especially for the first part of the relationship. They seem to devote all their time and efforts in making sure that all your needs are met.

- They can be incredible braggarts, talking about past successes and their grandiose plans for the future. Sociopath may also talk about their past lovers and how many people of the opposite sex are attracted to them. A sociopath will top it off with a comment that you're "special" and that's why he's with you despite the others chasing him.

- Sociopaths have no problem maintaining eye contact. Some people term this as "intense" eyes. People often break eye contact as a sign of self consciousness – something sociopaths aren't privy to.

- They might push you to provide for them. Sociopaths rarely see the need for hard work and would rather get the things they need through easier means. If the person is leeching off you, then something is definitely wrong.

- They can be excellent liars. If you catch a sociopath in a lie however, chances are you will be blamed for it. Some may point the finger towards others while some may change the subject entirely. However, a sociopath will never admit to the lie.

- Sociopaths are isolated and they want to do the same thing to you. This makes it easier for them to pick you out of the herd and basically turn into the center of your universe. They might make it seem as though you don't need any other relationships aside from theirs by valuing you to the extreme. However, this is only the first stage of the Sociopath Cycle: Idealize, Devalue, and Discard.

Note that the same signs may hold true if you think you're dating a psychopath. The difference between the two personalities is really very subtle unless pushed to the extremes.

Sociopath Parents

Sociopath parents are no different from psychopath parents. They vary from two mentally abusive extremes of "ignore" and "abuse". It is, therefore, not surprising that the children of sociopaths grow up with mental disorders themselves.

The typical sociopathic parents are lacking in moral compass. They completely disregard the feelings and rights of other people. In general, they are manipulative, insensitive, cold, dishonest and sneaky. They basically care about one person in the entire world and that is their selves.

Without a full range of human emotions, sociopaths hold nothing more than anger and self interest. People who are exposed to sociopaths, especially the children of disordered parents are among the most abusive and highly dysfunctional.

Not all sociopathic parents are the same however. It is also unfair to conclude that all sociopaths are criminals. In fact, a lot of sociopaths do not turn out as serial killers. Moreover, there is no single type among those who commit crimes.

While some sociopathic parents like to draw attention to themselves, others are simply indifferent. There are cold ones. They can be uncaring and extremely self-centered.

Most personality disordered parents have no genuine interest in their children. As a matter of fact, it is typical for them to become hurtful and abusive. They are more hurtful among those that are helpless and defenseless. They do not feel empathy. They may have little and more often than not, no consideration at all for others.

Children who grow up with mildly antisocial parents are luckier than those whose parents are heavily sociopathic. But one thing is for sure; children of sociopaths can be severely neglected. They can be cruelly beaten and emotionally abused. It is also typical of sociopathic parents to explode in fits of rage when they do not get exactly what they want.

Children of sociopathic parents are highly disempowered. The environment they are exposed to from a very early age is highly dysfunctional. They are denied of genuine care and strong support. These children may learn to cope with their disordered parent by hiding when the adults are angry. They will learn to smile at their parent's command, never because they are happy or delighted. Children of sociopaths learn to be watchful of their every move. They know it is the only way they can avoid becoming a target.

Children naturally love their parents. They may follow orders willingly just to gain approval. But soon enough, they will come to understand that their sociopathic parents do not and cannot truly care about them.

It is typical for children of sociopaths to be used, deceived and manipulated. They will likely grow up with little to no self esteem. All their growing up years, they have been frightened and threatened. They are likely to feel worthless and invisible. They carry deep scars and without the appropriate help, they are likely to carry the heavy emotional baggage all their lives.

Sociopaths in History

Ted Bundy – Ted Bundy has also been identified as a psychopath but bearing the differences of the personality order in mind, it can be argued that Ted Bundy is a sociopath. He exhibits all the obvious signs of sociopathy, the most powerful one being charm. Indeed, he was so charming that women still supported him during his trial for murder. At one point, he proposed marriage to one of the women testifying on his behalf. On his way to a successful political career, Ted Bundy was supremely confident every time he faced the media with his crimes, acting like he did nothing wrong. This facet of his personality also makes him a narcissist. Ted Bundy is believed to have killed at least 30 women, but the full count is not really known.

Steve Jobs – Although not really diagnosed with sociopathy, some people consider Steve Jobs as a sociopath or at least just a few symptoms short of being a full sociopath. There is no question that Steve Jobs has the charm – he was a brilliant marketing strategist that became the face of Apple for years. Behind the marketing face, however, it is said that Steve Jobs can be extensively cruel, often lashing out at employees until they give him what he wants. Unfortunately, Steve Jobs isn't always aware of the results he craves, but prefers to see and judge – ridiculing others in the process. Steve Jobs may also have a streak of narcissism as he liked to take credit for other's people's work, even in his field of marketing. Others see his lack of empathy in his denial of his first child, even going so far as to announcing his sterility. It was only years later (after having more children) that Jobs finally acknowledged his first child's existence.

Chapter 10: Beware, Telltale Signs of a Psychopath and Sociopath

Psychopaths and sociopaths are dangerous people. The antisocial individual in your life may not be a serial killer but the emotional scar this person will leave you can be quite deep. Have you been hurt real bad by someone? Has someone made you feel worthless? Have you ever felt used? And do you have suspicions about this individual's real personality? That said, here are the most common signs of a psychopath and sociopath.

Is that person charming?

Not everyone who demonstrates great charisma is sociopaths or psychopaths. But antisocial disordered individuals can have charming personalities. As a matter of fact, they can easily attract a following. People seem to like being around them especially individuals who are desperate for guidance and direction. That's because sociopaths and psychopaths give them exactly what they need. They can be anything or anyone they want to be, at least on the surface. They will act if that's what needs to be done to get what they ultimately want.

In order to get people on their side, sociopathic and psychopathic men and women will make others believe just how wonderful they are. Sometimes, they act like they are the victims. How do they do these when they are incapable of feeling like normal people do? They are keen observers of human behavior. They take time in reading people's weaknesses, and they know exactly how to exploit such weaknesses.

Sociopaths and psychopaths are everywhere. They can be anyone from a street hustler to a crooked salesman. They can even be businesspeople. It is quite easy for them to trick and play with other people's emotions. They will take advantage of others, and they are masters of deflecting responsibility to everyone else, whoever is convenient to blame.

Sociopaths and psychopaths can appear sexy too. They are likely to possess strong sexual attractiveness. Again, this is not to say that all sexy people have the disorder. What you need to watch out for are those individuals who seem to have weird fetishes and voracious sexual appetites.

Does the person you suspect have a huge ego?

Delusions of grandeur are common among psychopaths and sociopaths. Their sense of self is extremely inflated that they remain unfazed despite heavy criticism. They also feel like they are entitled. They think they are deserving of amazing things. They are well deserved even if they do not work for it.

It is typical for antisocial individuals to have an unrealistic view of their talents and skills. For instance, this person may not have the voice but thinks he or she deserves a singing contract. Psychopathic and sociopathic individuals also think they are better than everyone else.

More often than not, they are narcissistic too. Their favorite topic is their selves. No one else matters in their world. No one deserves the spotlight more than they do.

Does this person have exceptional acting skills?

They are great con artists. Many polished con artists are more likely psychopathic or sociopathic. They are well capable of deceiving people. They can get into character and they are flawless in playing the part. They are quite skillful at fooling others. While they pretend to be sensitive, caring, generous and dutiful, they are already taking advantage of you.

Psychopaths and sociopaths are so good at what they do to the point of believing it themselves. When they are caught red handed, they will stand by their disguise. They would even act as if they are unjustly accused even in the face of strong evidence. When there seems to be no other way out, they may admit to their wrongdoing but even then, they will fake contrition. They would even plead incessantly for forgiveness. It is typical for them to plead on pity. But then, they move on to conning others. They will do this for the rest of their lives.

Does he or she think about no one else?

To a psychopath or a sociopath, there is no one more important than their own selves. All they care about is self gratification. They consider life to be a mere game in which other people are only objects to be played with and used so they can get what they want.

Is this person impulsive?

These people have no regard for consequences. They have very poor impulse control. Most of them are aggressive. They tend to lash out without warning.

Does this individual have no respect for rules?

Rules are merely constraints. These people do not just find ways to bend the rules, they break them. Regardless if it is a law or a social rule or a reasonable expectation from people around them, antisocial people simply do not care. They will violate anything and anyone as long as it serves their purpose. They will blatantly break the rules when no one is watching. To avoid getting caught, they blend in pretty well. Others will even brag about it.

They seem to be very intelligent.

Sociopaths and psychopaths may seem normal. They seem to possess superior human qualities. They talk a lot and often. This will give other people the impression that they are quite knowledgeable with plenty of genuine interests. This also makes them desirable and interesting to the eyes of potential victims.

Does it seem strange that this person you suspect does not worry?

When other people will be stuck in the same disturbing situation, they will be extremely stressed out. Antisocial individuals however, do not seem to feel anxiety or worry. They are always composed and poised. They seem to be oozing with confidence. They are exceptionally calm even in the direst of situations.

Their response to psychiatric institutions and prison may be different however. When they feel like they have lost two of the most important things to them, freedom and control, they become uneasy. Their uneasiness is not driven by remorse, guilt or any other emotion. Rather, it comes solely from external circumstances.

Is he or she totally unreliable?

These people may give the impression of being the most reliable in the planet. However, it eventually becomes evident that they completely lack any sense of responsibility. They will make promises only to break them. Taking responsibility is simply not their forte. Even when they are confronted, they will not change a thing about their ways.

The only thing psychopaths and sociopaths are good at is creating the impression of reliability. But the truth is they are very unreliable whether in serious or trivial matters.

Does he or she lie constantly and convincingly?

It is quite remarkable how antisocial people lack any regard for the truth. It is impossible and not advisable to trust in whatever comes out of a psychopath or a sociopath's mouth. They are so good at lying that they can be very convincing. Their lies become the truth. They can look people in the eye and tell an outright lie, and they will continue to lie to get what they want. They still lie when they are caught lying. They often use lies to cover up their acts.

Is this person never to blame?

Psychopaths and sociopaths do not feel humiliated. The feelings of shame and regret are foreign to them. This is what makes them well capable of committing horrible things against other people.

When they are confronted, they put others on the line. They are quick to point fingers and pretend like they are the unfortunate victims. It is never the psychopath or sociopath's fault. They always find someone else to blame.

Does this person never seem to learn?

While antisocial individuals may appear rational, they are in truth, the exact opposite of what they portray. They are likely to throw away excellent opportunities especially at changing their ways. They do not care if they have been caught and punished before. They will continue on doing the same things and sticking with the same behavior. Punishment will not change them. In fact, experts do not believe anything will.

Does this person make uninterrupted eye contact?

Another typical characteristic of antisocial people is their ability to give intense and uninterrupted eye contact. They are capable of staring without feeling uncomfortable. These people think it is what can get them what they want.

Does this person work hard to isolate you?

Meeting people is the kind of thing sociopaths and psychopaths like doing. When they meet a potential victim, they move in swiftly. They do not give the other person a chance to change his or her mind and pull back. This is especially true for a psychopath or a sociopath who wants to be romantically involved with you.

If this is the case then this person may make you feel like you are soul mates. They are so good at mimicking emotions and observing people that they will say all the right things at the right time. He or she will shower you with adoration, attention and affection. This person will make you feel like he or she wants to be with you all the time. They also make sure no one else gets in the way. So this person is likely to isolate you from your friends and family.

Does this person flip like a switch?

If the person you suspect makes you feel cared for one minute and worthless on the next, he or she may in fact be a sociopath or a psychopath. They flip fast like switches often leaving you confused and broken.

Does he or she make you feel sorry?

Another tactic psychopaths and sociopaths resort to is the pity play. They like to appeal to other people's sympathy. They make you feel sorry for their financial setbacks, psychotic ex or abusive childhood experience. They play their cards and they do it so well you'd fall for their web of lies.

Why do they do what they do?

For normal people, the affection and bond with others have a strong influence on their purpose. Unfortunately, the sociopath and the psychopath do not feel love and other human emotions. Such do not give them purpose. All they care about is winning.

Life is a game they play. Everyone else is a chess piece they manipulate. Antisocial people work for a single purpose—to win. And they will do anything and stop at nothing to win.

They are conniving and clever. They have all the time to scheme and come up with crafty ways to deceive people. That's because they are not bothered by any other concerns like relationships, conflicting feeling and moral dilemmas. They do not have any of those to worry about. The only thing that may concern them is boredom.

Getting bored easily is a problem for psychopaths and sociopaths which is why they constantly look for stimulation. And boredom comes easily because they do not have other things to occupy their minds except for playing a game. And playing to win the game can become dull. So they seek constant stimulation, even negative ones like drama.

Chapter 11: How to Cope with the Sociopath or Psychopath in Your Life

It is emotionally draining to be with a personality disordered individual. It can change you for the worse. But dealing with them is not that easy either. Take note of the following tips to better cope with these disordered individuals.

Understand that these people are not like you or I.

The first thing you need to do is to understand what goes on in the mind of a psychopath or sociopath. You need to accept the fact that this person is not capable of caring for anyone else. For these individuals, other people are meant to be used for their own selfish gains. Morality and kindness are foreign to these people. In fact, they are disgusted by it. If you adhere to such things, you are considered an idiot.

You do not matter to this person and probably never will. More importantly, psychopaths and sociopaths think that their victims do deserve what they get for being idiots allowing themselves to be used and abused.

Avoid them.

You can never win with a sociopath or psychopath. In which case, it is best to avoid them. That is the only way you can protect yourself from being hurt immensely. Quit them cold turkey. When this person feels like he or she has lost his or her effect on you, it is likely the person will let go and move on to another victim. The only way to be free from this unhealthy relationship is to stop being the victim.

Show the person you have nothing to offer.

A psychopath or sociopath use people for various reasons. They may want access to your connections, to your financial resources or they simply think you are a solution to their boredom. If you want them to stop pestering you then you should show them you have nothing more to offer.

If money is what they are after, make sure to hide your money where it is impossible for them to find. Put it in the bank and hide your bank statements. Do not give away any signs that you have money.

But what if you have to live or work with these people?

What if the psychopath or sociopath is a co-worker or a family member? How are you supposed to deal with them? It is not plain and simple but here are a few suggestions on how to make life easier.

Speak quickly and often.

These individuals are in constant need of stimulation since they hate boredom. You would not want to stir dislike from this person but you should know it is impossible to win his or her favor as well. So one of the safest things to do is to speak quickly and often with them. Speak as agreeably as possible.

Be generous with complements.

You will never win with these types of people. You would not want to stir trouble either. When they try to speak to you, engage in the conversation. Agree with them politely. Give them compliments too. There is nothing you can do to downsize the person's ego so just feed it.

Avoid silent pauses.

When you speak to the person, he or she is more likely to find a way around you, get to you, and manipulate you in any way he or she can. To avoid this situation, do not leave any silent pauses. Keep talking too. And when the person tries to work his or her charms, quickly change the subject and keep changing it. It will surely throw him or her off the game. And as soon as you can, excuse yourself.

It's all about being neutral and safe.

Stick to neutral and safe topics like the weather, sports, and news. Never discuss your personal life. Do not give the person any information he or she can use against you later on. Avoid sharing emotional stuff. Do not give this person any more reason to manipulate you.

Do not try to change them.

At some point, a person will never change. Psychopaths and sociopaths in general lack the ability to change for the reason of being better. They will not and see no reason why change is necessary. And they will not certainly change for you. So, do not even bother.

Finally, you should realize it is not your fault. Learn to forgive yourself and move on. When you have been exposed to the ways of a sociopath or psychopath for a long time, it will be extremely helpful to seek therapy.

Chapter 12: Children with Antisocial Tendencies

Adults are usually diagnosed with these two disorders. Such illnesses may begin to manifest in early childhood. Kids with sociopathic and psychopathic tendencies usually show several behavioral problems. If parents fail to control and help their kids at this early point, there is a great chance the child will grow up to be either a sociopath or psychopath.

Signs of sociopathy and psychopathy can be detected in children as young as 7 years of age. Therapists, however, are reluctant in making a definite diagnosis until said child reaches 18 years of age. In a documentary "Child of Rage", a girl heading towards a sociopathic path underwent treatment and evidently "cured" of her sociopathic tendencies. Hence, this suggests that with early action, the said condition can be prevented.

It is normal for parents with best intentions to avoid associating their children with conduct disorder or antisocial traits. In fact, most parents will deny even the most outright signs. This is a sensitive topic and one which parents may try to avoid, but denying it can be much more aggravating for the child especially in the future.

If you suspect your child to show sociopathic or psychopathic tendencies, what are you ought to do? Most parents may just disregard it and move on crossing their fingers that these behavioral tendencies in their children are nothing but a phase. But is it?

For a sensitive and controversial topic as this, it is important to be in the best frame of mind first. And so, here are a few reminders.

Please withhold any moral judgment.

Experts have not laid out reasons why a person may engage in sociopathic behaviors. A young individual may steal for various reasons. It could be because of peer pressure, thrill seeking behavior, anger or impulsivity. In other words, while the end behavior may be determined, it is quite difficult to define the intentions and ultimately know what goes on in the young person's heart and mind. In which case, it is important that you withhold moral judgment with regard to these behaviors. In order to help your child, you must practice objectivity.

Psychopathy and sociopathy is dynamic.

There are young people who have been identified with antisocial disorder tendencies, received appropriate treatment and do exceptionally well later on in their lives. While a kid may bully others mercilessly, assault their parents or even spend some time behind bars, it does not mean they are hopeless cases. Some of these kids make it through college. Some of them are able to build a sense of spirituality and build meaningful relationships. They can even become caretakers of other people. The truth is children who show antisocial tendencies are dynamic. Every person, young or old, must be held accountable for their bad behaviors. They must face the consequences of their actions. However, adults especially parents should avoid static judgments. While it is important to become objective and realistic, you must also hold on to hope.

This is not an all or nothing case.

Children who demonstrate antisocial behaviors can be thoughtful, considerate, and judicious too. They may even show concern for the feelings and rights of their peers. What parents should watch out for is an inconsistency in demonstrating such forethought and concern.

Most parents ignore the signs because they see their children defending another child from a bully that one time. They think that by demonstrating such concern, it is virtually impossible for their kid to have antisocial tendencies. Before such conclusion should be made, an in-depth study of behavioral patterns as well as the child's psychology is very much needed. That is the only way to determine whether or not a child has antisocial personality or the tendency of developing one.

Sociopathy and psychopathy exist on a spectrum.

Children who demonstrate antisocial traits are not necessarily on the extreme statistically. In fact, young people with conduct disorder who engaged in stealing and lying do not meet the antisocial personality criteria outrightly. The number of children who display antisocial characteristics may be greater than you think.

Psychopathy and sociopathy can be inherited.

Experts recognize three main factors that cause these personality disorders. One of them is genetics. This does not necessarily mean your family is crazy or that it is your fault. The truth is traits tend to differ in magnitude between generations. At times too, psychopathy and sociopathy can come out of nowhere. At the same time, if any of the biological parents of the child demonstrate sociopathic or psychopathic traits, the tendency of the child becoming one is much greater. Either way, it is a point worth considering. Again, objectivity is very important in giving your child appropriate support.

The other two possible causes of these personality disorders are environment and trauma. Children who are exposed to antisocial behaviors may develop the tendency as well. Such influence may not only come from parents. Exposure to peers showing violent behavior may also result to the development of psychopathic or sociopathic behavior in a child.

It is also possible for children who had a traumatic experience in life to develop psychopathic and sociopathic tendencies. An accident, death of a loved one, abuse and other similar experiences may also push a child to the edge.

Now the question is – what are the signs of a sociopath child? Here are some symptoms:

- Hyperactivity
- vandalism
- Issues with sustaining relationship with peers
- Recklessness and an obvious disregard for the safety of others including self
- Cruelty to animals
- Compulsive lying
- Vandalism
- Stealing

- Disregard for the safety of others

- Fascination with fire

- Getting into lots of fights due to aggressiveness

- Disregard and anger towards persons of authority

- Speech problems

- Learning disorder

- Persistent bedwetting, even after 5 years of age

- Lack of remorse for wrongdoing

- Irritability and aggressiveness, often engaging in assaults and physical fights

- Manipulation

- Showing contempt for people who try to understand them

Antisocial tendencies in children may show similarities with the symptoms as observed in adults. However, there are signs specifically and increasingly observed in young people. Such includes bullying, cruelty to animals and stealing among others.

Some of these symptoms as listed above may be a mere part of the child's growing up process. However, there are specific behavioral traits that help indicate sociopathic and psychopathic tendencies. Psychiatrists do believe that plenty of diagnosed adults have demonstrated sociopathic and psychopathic signs during their childhood. And so it cannot be more emphasized just how important it is to be observant and vigilant when it concerns children.

Is it possible to cure a psychopathic or sociopathic child?

It can prove very difficult. Treatment requires a long time. It calls for patience. But according to research, several effective treatments are available and it can be extremely helpful.

A child with antisocial tendencies requires constant adult supervision and unconditional parental support. Parents who suspect their children of these tendencies should work at building a bond of trust and establishing a strong companionship with their kids. All these help when it comes to preventing sociopathic and psychopathic tendencies in children from fully developing.

Interventions and treatments including impulse control counseling and other psychotherapy methods that aim to teach young people the essential skills necessary for them to understand and respect societal norms prove beneficial. There are cases when medication may apply. Such may work to supplement psychotherapy and counseling sessions.

The bottom line is avoidance is not the solution. Behavioral problems can be more than simply an act of rebellion. Dealing with these problems requires personal, emotional and professional help. Although it may be difficult to admit your child has a problem, you must face the facts. Otherwise, it may be too late.

Do not leave the issue untreated. Such will only make the child feel abandoned and neglected. The issue does not solve itself. Never let your child deal with it alone or worse, with the wrong people. Otherwise, it will only serve to aggravate the child's sociopathic tendencies.

Chapter 13: Frequently Asked Questions

Are most sociopaths and psychopaths male?

Although many of the popular sociopaths and psychopaths fall within the male gender, this is not always the case. There are also females who have been diagnosed with this personality disorder, albeit they are often harder to pin down. A good example of a female with key signs of a sociopath/psychopath is Elizabeth Bathory, dubbed as the female Dracula and rumored to have killed more than 300 women during her time.

Are all psychopaths and sociopaths criminals?

Some have commented that psychopaths and sociopaths are identified depending on whether they have crossed moral grounds or not. According to some people, "psychopath" is the term used for those who have committed a crime while "sociopath" is for people with the same symptoms but without committing criminal acts.

Unfortunately, it's not as simple as it sounds. The fact is that the two are highly different from each other and both are more than capable of transcending moral grounds – the only difference is the way they do it.

To answer the question – no, not everyone diagnosed as psychopaths and sociopaths turn into criminals. In fact, there are several high-profile people believed to be sociopaths including Donald Trump.

What professions contain the most psychopaths?

Further proof that not all psychopaths are destructive is their presence in different thriving industries. According to studies, some of professions with the most psychopaths include: lawyers, public servants, journalists, surgeons, police officers, media personalities and CEOs. Of course, that doesn't mean that everyone falling within this category is a psychopath/sociopath.

What professions contain the most narcissists?

As explained before, businessmen and cult leaders are some of the most attractive positions for narcissists. However, you might also find them in: show business, medical profession, politics and law enforcement.

Are sociopaths capable of living normal lives?

Yes. The myth is that all sociopaths are sadistic killers – which aren't entirely true. Many of them are living normal lifestyles with respect to cultural norms. In fact, many of them are successful. They are not psychotic or delusional but rather, have a very different way of thinking and therefore different approach to many of life's problems. A sociopath's constant need for excitement and stimulation is one of the reasons why some of them resort to violent acts in an attempt to push the norms. In today's society however, there are numerous outlets for excitement that are both healthy and respectful of other people's rights.

What MBTI type is most likely to be a narcissist, sociopath or psychopath?

MBTI or Myerrs Briggs Type Indicator is one of the most popular methods used to test the personality of an individual. A long-standing system, MBTI was actually used by companies to determine the employability of people seeking work in their company. Despite the accuracy of MBTI in personality aspects however, it is believed the psychopaths and sociopaths belong to an entirely different personality type altogether. Therefore, assigning them letters using the MBTI credentials is inaccurate. Still, there are those who insist that the system works and the best personality type for sociopaths and psychopaths are INTJ, ISTJ, and ISTP.

One thing you should understand about sociopaths, psychopaths and narcissists is that despite all the negative connotations – it might not be as bad as it seems. Like the brain, there is still so much we don't know about this personality disorder, which is why generalizations cannot always be made. Today, research is being done to further find out more about people with this condition and exactly what this entails.

Conclusion

Thank you again for purchasing this book!

I hope this book was able to help you to learn more about the different personality disorders, specifically the narcissistic mind and the psychopaths/sociopaths.

The next step is to read up on the different people who have been diagnosed with these conditions. Keep in mind that personality disorders are not cookie-cutter type, making each person and story unique.

Finally, if you enjoyed this book, please take the time to share your thoughts and post a review on Amazon. We do our best to reach out to readers and provide the best value we can. Your positive review will help us achieve that. It'd be greatly appreciated!

Thank you and good luck!

Check Out My Other Books

Below you'll find some of my other popular books that are popular on Amazon and Kindle as well. Simply click on the links below to check them out. Alternatively, you can visit my author page on Amazon to see other work done by me.

Cure For Controlling People: The Ultimate Guide for Releasing You from Those That Control You In A Relationship

http://www.amazon.com/Cure-Controlling-People-Relationship-Codependency-ebook/dp/B00JOHTV5K

ADHD Symptom and Strategies: The Ultimate Guide for Understanding and Handling Attention Deficit Disorder in Adults and Children

http://www.amazon.com/ADHD-Symptom-Strategies-Understanding-Hyperactivity-ebook/dp/B00JOZT3DM

Narcissism Unleashed 2nd Edition! The Ultimate Guide to Understanding the Mind of a Narcissist, Sociopath and Psychopath!

http://www.amazon.com/Narcissism-Understanding-Narcissist-Narcissistic-Personality-ebook/dp/B00JP0UQM8

How to Cure the Workaholic Addiction: Control Anxiety and Stress Before It's Too Late!

http://www.amazon.com/How-Cure-Workaholic-Addiction-Workaholics-ebook/dp/B00JPZJY2Q/

Living with Autism: The Successful Steps to Recognizing, Adapting, Learning, and Understanding Autism http://www.amazon.com/Living-Autism-Recognizing-Understanding-Breakthrough-ebook/dp/B00JQS6Z5Q

The Ultimate Self Esteem Guide: Steps to Building Self Esteem, Confidence, and Inner strength!

http://www.amazon.com/Ultimate-Self-Esteem-Guide-Codependancy-ebook/dp/B00JY2F3K2

The Shopping Addiction: A Cure for Compulsive Shopping and Spending to Free Yourself from Addiction!

http://www.amazon.com/Shopping-Addiction-Compulsive-Self-Help-Impulsive-ebook/dp/B00JY2FYDS

Living With OCD: A Powerful Guide To Understanding Obsessive Compulsive Disorder In Children And Adults

http://www.amazon.com/Living-OCD-Understanding-Compulsive-Personality-ebook/dp/B00K3E3E06

BOX SET #1: Narcissism Unleashed! & Cure For Controlling People

http://www.amazon.com/BOX-SET-Controlling-Narcissistic-Codependency-ebook/dp/B00KAATSFI

BOX SET #2: Narcissism Unleashed! & Mind Control Mastery

http://www.amazon.com/BOX-SET-Narcissistic-Personality-Manifestation-ebook/dp/B00K9URU9O

BOX SET #3 ADHD Symptoms & Strategies & Living With OCD

http://www.amazon.com/Symptoms-Strategies-Attention-attention-hyperactivity-ebook/dp/B00KA0K4SI

BOX SET #4: Living With OCD & The Ultimate Self Esteem Guide

http://www.amazon.com/BOX-SET-Ultimate-Confidence-Strength-ebook/dp/B00KA0U04G

BOX SET #5: Narcissism Unleashed! & Mind Control Mastery & The Shopping Addiction & Living With OCD & The Ultimate Self Esteem Guide

http://www.amazon.com/Box-Set-Narcissism-Compulsive-Psychopath-ebook/dp/B00KK96T56

www.ingramcontent.com/pod-product-compliance
Lightning Source LLC
Chambersburg PA
CBHW060200290526
45789CB00003B/1102